The Challenge of Revival

Fairmeadow
Books

Paul Young

© 2006 Paul Young
ISBN 0-9523478-6-5

Published in Great Britain.

All rights reserved.

No part of this publication may be reproduced or transmitted, in any form by any means, electronic or mechanical, including photocopying, recording, or any information storage and retrieval system, without permission in writing.

Printed by:
Bible Studies Institute,
Lower Glenageary Road, Dun Loaghaire, Co. Dublin, Ireland

Contents

Foreword · · · · · · · · · · · · · · · · · · · 5

Introduction · · · · · · · · · · · · · · · · · 7

The Commencement of Revival · · · · · · · · · · · · · 9

The Explosive Power of Revival · · · · · · · · · · · · 19

The Rise and Fall of the Revival · · · · · · · · · · · 29

The Conditions for Revival · · · · · · · · · · · · · 39

Further Reading · · · · · · · · · · · · · · · · 57

Books by Paul Young · · · · · · · · · · · · · · · 59

About the Author · · · · · · · · · · · · · · · · 61

Foreword

'Christ will be Christ,' wrote Samuel Rutherford, 'in the dregs and refuse of men.' And thank God that it is so! Time and again He reaches down into our 'dregs and refuse' and, with irresistible kindness, pours over us what we so desperately need yet never deserve: healing, forgiveness and love. But at special times – and what times! – men and women in their thousands together are dignified by this divine touch, families are mended, communities healed and nations reformed. This is 'revival', and how right to call it so, for these, and these only, are the times when we truly 'live again'. It is to these times – and to one time in particular – that Paul Young has devoted his considerable skill in the pages that follow.

I have known Paul for many years and watched with pleasure as he has developed into the respected church leader he is today. I honour him as a man of God, and I honour his passionate commitment to see the full scope and diversity of God's blessings in Christ brought to our nation. His own personal life and his influential ministry are dedicated to that purpose.

In this booklet Paul inspires and challenges us with a great revival that rocked his own nation of Wales a little over a century ago. He speaks of great events that lift and warm our hearts. But there is more here than just the retelling of a great spiritual tale, however good that may be for us to hear. It is today, not yesterday, that Paul is most concerned about, and that we should learn not only from others' experiences but from our own, just how great and wonderful our God is. So he gives us timeless principles as well as timely warnings which, if we faithfully follow them, must help – God willing – to bring the day of God's next great outpouring many steps closer, and make us more ready for it when it arrives. There is much here for us all to learn and put into practice.

May it not be long before other writers can look back on our day and tell the tale of how we too were soaked in the Spirit of revival. In the meantime, men like Paul Young are pointing faithfully to that great hope. We do well to follow their lead. Revive Thy work, O Lord!

Dr. David Tucker

Worldwide President of Trans World Radio

Introduction

There was a great deal of excitement in the Principality of Wales in the year 2004 as an event from one hundred years earlier was commemorated. That event lasted for several months and went on into 1905, affecting people in all parts of the country. The event, of course, was the Welsh Revival and it helped to transform the spiritual landscape of Wales and also ripples of that event were eventually felt around the globe.

I was asked to deliver two messages on the Welsh Revival for a conference in Cardiff and subsequently I have given those lectures in a number of places. I later transformed the material into five radio talks for the programme 'Truth for Today' which is broadcast on Sky Digital 888 by Trans World Radio. Also I have worked the material into a short article for the magazine 'Precious Seed'.

It is felt that there might be some benefit in putting the material into a more permanent format thus allowing it to be more widely distributed. This book attempts to be both factual and challenging. It is not good enough to simply rejoice in what God did many years ago but we need to take up the challenge of living in expectation of another pouring out of God's Spirit and to be in the right spiritual condition that such an outpouring is actually possible.

My thanks to all who made this work a possibility and it goes forward with the prayer that God's people will be blessed and challenged.

Paul Young

Chapter 1

The Commencement of Revival

In 1904, just over one hundred years ago, the Principality of Wales was rocked and deeply altered by a great outpouring of the Spirit of God. It was a phenomenon that became known as 'The Welsh Revival'. Remarkable and astounding events took place, with hundreds and thousands of people being influenced and changed during those weeks and months of revival and eventually the whole world was spiritually touched as a result of what took place in that small Principality. There have recently been a number of publications both in written and visual forms that have commemorated the events of a century ago and enabled them to become real to a new generation of Christian people.

Unfortunately the contrast with the present spiritual conditions in Wales could hardly be greater. Today we are witnessing many churches and chapels in serious decline with dwindling numbers in attendance and many buildings closing their doors as places of worship. The church of the twenty-first century in the Western world is materially rich but spiritually impoverished. Too often energy is consumed on selfish ambitions, bitter infighting, petty jealousies and self-centred pride. The church appears to be making little impact upon a society that is sliding into ever increasing immorality and that is becoming less and less Christian in emphasis. The modern church

The Challenge of Revival

lacks an awareness of the presence of God and the power of prayer seems muted. Thus the power and anointing of the Holy Spirit is rarely seen and forward progress, both numerically and spiritually, seems stunted.

Do we really want to pay the price for revival?

As we look back upon the Welsh Revival it must never be with a shallow sentimentality that such times would return. We must face the challenge of revival and ask: "Do we really want to pay the price? Do we truly want to purge our lives of everything that grieves God and limits the work of the Holy Spirit?" There is a price to be paid for revival and it is not abundantly clear that the modern church has any desire or willingness to pay that price, which in personal terms could be great. Yet revival is important to the survival of the Christian Gospel in Wales and is obviously a vital need today. The events of the Welsh Revival leave us awestruck and make us wonder at the greatness of God and also the great things that He can achieve in the lives of individuals and of society as a whole during times of revival.

What is Revival?

In order to gain an insight into what is meant by revival, it is worth looking at a few of the many definitions – given over the years.

1. ***Jonathan Edwards*** the great American preacher of the eighteenth century, who witnessed and wrote about the revival

The Commencement of Revival

known as "The Great Awakening" said that Revival is: "God's major means of extending His kingdom".

2. ***Edwin Orr***, who has researched and written extensively on revivals, says that Revival is "a movement of the Holy Spirit bringing about a Revival in New Testament Christianity in the church of Christ and its related community."

3. ***Duncan Campbell*** who witnessed the wonder of "the Hebrides Revival" in the Scottish western isles during 1949 described revival as "a community saturated with God".

A community saturated with God

4. ***Charles Haddon Spurgeon***, the great nineteenth century Baptist preacher who saw continuous revival during his ministry at the Metropolitan Tabernacle in the Elephant and Castle area of London, said, "A true revival is looked for in the church."

5. ***Rhys Bevan Jones*** in 1904 in Wales said that revival is "the church on its knees". Indeed this concept was a sort of slogan of the Welsh Revival and was formulated as "bend the church and save the people".

6. ***Peterus Octavianus*** who witnessed the 1973 revival in Borneo said: "Revivals do not begin happily with everyone having a good time. They start with a broken and contrite heart."

7. ***Brian Edwards*** whose book *Revival* is a classic wrote, "Re-

The Challenge of Revival

vival is the awakening of the church, making it holy and alive once again", and "Revival highlights the big issues that unite Christians, rather than the secondary issues that divide."

8. ***Powell Parry*** saw revival as "the presence of God – everywhere."

So revival is a work of God's Spirit to breathe new life and vitality into the church and it was gloriously seen in Wales in 1904. Yet this was not the first time that revival had been experienced in the Principality. Revival had come in the 1500s and again in the 1730s with the leaders being Howell Harris and Daniel Rowlands. There was a revival in the North Wales town of Bala in 1791 with Thomas Charles; in the west coast town of Aberystwyth in 1805, in Beddgelert in 1817; and a nationwide revival in 1859 with David Morgan as one of the notable leaders. The nation seems to have regularly experienced the wonder of revival and we are now living in one of the longest periods of time without a revival since Christianity first came to Wales. It should be a deep challenge to us and we need to be burdened for another visitation of God's Spirit.

Evan Roberts

In 1904 the man used by God to usher in revival was a former coal miner named Evan Roberts.

At the beginning of the twentieth century there was a small explosion in a South Wales coal mine. One of the results was that some of the pages of a Bible were scorched. Apparently the pages were 2 Chronicles 6 where the words of Solomon are recorded as he prayed for Re-

The Commencement of Revival

vival. The owner of the Bible was Evan Roberts who was destined by God to light the flames of Revival in the country of Wales. Pictures of that scorched Bible went around the world following the amazing events of 1904.

Evan Roberts was one of fourteen children and was born on the 8th June 1878 in Loughor a small town to the west of Swansea. He was just twenty-six years old when he was used by God to bring Revival to Wales. Initially he worked as a coal miner and then as a blacksmith. At the age of thirteen or fourteen he had been counselled by a deacon of Moriah Chapel named William Davies never to miss a prayer meeting. He was warned that he should never be absent in case the Holy Spirit came and Evan would then have felt like the apostle Thomas who was elsewhere when the newly risen Christ first appeared to His disciples. Evan Roberts heeded the advice and never missed a prayer meeting or any other meeting for that matter.

Evan Roberts started to attend school in the Cardiganshire town of Newcastle Emlyn and it was from there, on Thursday, 29th September 1904, he went to a Chapel service in Blaenannerch. At the close of the service the preacher, Seth Joshua, offered a prayer and in the course of it said, "Bend us, O Lord!" The idea behind such a sentiment is that we should be bent or moulded to the will of God. This had a powerful impact upon Evan Roberts and it gripped his heart and mind. He is said to have fallen to his knees in prayer, leaning over the back of the pew in front of him and repeatedly prayed, "Bend me! Bend me! Bend me!" The perspiration that stood out on his face joined the tears that flowed. It was a mighty and memorable moment in the life of that young man.

Bend us, O Lord

The Challenge of Revival

It would seem that he stayed in that condition for a long time, with people coming to comfort him and wipe his face. He was essentially overwhelmed by three things. Firstly, the love of God seemed to forcibly impinge upon his mind. Secondly his own unworthiness humbled him and powerfully affected him. Thirdly, he was overwhelmed with a burden for the salvation of lost souls. He was certainly deeply moved and radically changed by the experience and he referred to that time as "Blaenannerch's great meeting."

That gathering might have been the critical turning point but it did not come out of the blue because for many years Evan Roberts had been reading, talking and thinking about revival. It was constantly on his mind and in his prayers and he conversed often on the subject, especially with his great friend Sydney Evans. It is reported that one night Evan Roberts came into the school building after having spent time in prayer with God in the garden and his face shone to the point of glowing. Sydney Evans was utterly taken aback but Roberts said, "I have got wonderful news for you. I had a vision of all Wales being lifted up to Heaven. We are going to see the mightiest Revival that Wales has ever known – the Holy Spirit is coming just now. We must be ready. We must have a little band and go all over the country preaching." The words sound almost breathlessly hysterical but they proved to be prophetic. There was an intense passion in the heart of Evan Roberts for Revival and he had such deep times of communion and fellowship with God that sometimes he was overwhelmed with the presence of the Almighty.

All Wales being lifted up to Heaven

The Commencement of Revival

The Diary of Revival

31st October 1904: Evan Roberts felt a strong leading from the Lord to return to his home town of Loughor. When he arrived he told his mother, "There will be a great change in Loughor in less than a fortnight. We are going to have the greatest revival that Wales has ever seen."

1st November 1904: Evan Roberts spoke to the young people in the Chapel about the importance of being filled with the Spirit.

2nd November 1904: Evan Roberts spoke on the four great principles which all must follow who desire the outpouring of the Spirit.

1. Confess all known sin – those past sins must be put away and cleansed. This is the deep pursuit of holiness.

2. Remove everything that is doubtful from your life and forgive everybody – no one must be excluded.

3. Obey the prompting of the Holy Spirit – obedience must be instant, total and unquestioning.

4. Make public confession of Christ as your Saviour – be open in your allegiance to Christ.

Meetings continued throughout the week and the following Sunday, 6th November 1904 sixty young people responded in faith and repentance to the call of the Gospel.

7th November 1904: The Chapel was packed and people were moved to tears, while others cried out in agony of soul over their sins. For the first time the *Revival Love Song* was sung. The first line in Welsh is:

The Challenge of Revival

"Dyma gariad fel y moroedd" and in English, "Here is love, vast as the ocean". The meeting did not finish until 3.00a.m..

9th November 1904: The people of Loughor awoke to the footsteps of multitudes making their way to the early morning (6.00a.m) prayer meeting.

10th November 1904: The Western Mail carried reports of crowds flocking to the Chapel in Loughor.

11th November 1904: The service at Moriah Chapel was overflowing with over eight hundred people in attendance.

12th November 1904: From all the surrounding countryside, people flooded into Loughor and filled Moriah Chapel where Evan Roberts was preaching and also Pisgah Chapel where Sydney Evans was the preacher.

14th November 1904: Evan Roberts was preaching in Aberdare and one thousand people attended Ebenezer Congregational Chapel to hear him preach.

15th November 1904: The whole of Aberdare was stirred and the early morning prayer meeting lasted for four hours. There were immense crowds in the evening and during the service Evan Roberts gave out the hymn: "Heavenly Jesus ride victorious, Gird thy sword upon thy thigh." It is reported that instantly prayer and praise broke out in a spontaneous desire to worship God and that Evan Roberts walked amongst the congregation clapping his hands in what has been described as "holy ecstasy".

This was the beginning of what James Alexander Stewart called, "The Invasion of Wales by the Spirit through Evan Roberts."

The Commencement of Revival

God's Spirit broke upon the preacher

Evan Roberts then travelled up and down the South Wales Industrial Valleys preaching and conducting services and great spiritual anointing was experienced. There were many manifestations of the presence of the Holy Spirit. In addition to the ministry of Evan Roberts there was also the *Keswick in Wales* convention that year when God's Spirit broke upon the preacher F.B. Meyer and a similar thing happened to R.A. Torrey who was conducting a mission in the city of Cardiff. It has even been reported that meetings continued with passionate prayer after the preachers and ministers had left their churches and returned home for some rest.

Whitaker in his book *Great Revivals* writes: "The presence of God was felt everywhere. The atmosphere was divinely charged." People seem to have been convicted of sin and become aware of the need of salvation, even without the presence of a preacher or evangelist. In my home town of Maesteg it is reported that two coal miners had just come off the afternoon shift and were walking down Victoria Street at about 10.30p.m.. They had flagons of drink and were on their way home when they were suddenly aware of the presence of God, right there in the street. They knelt on the road and cried to God for mercy. Then they got up and ran down the steps to the nearest Chapel, where there were people inside praying. Those men, with deep contrition and not a little anxiety, wanted to be saved. Apparently such awareness of the awesomeness of God's presence was not unusual in the times of revival in Wales in 1904. As a footnote that Chapel to which they ran has now closed, been demolished and a house stands in its place.

The Challenge of Revival

The atmosphere was divinely charged

We may not be living in times of revival today but we can live in personal and daily revival no matter what goes on around us. We can read God's Word and spend good quality time in prayer with our Saviour. Our souls can daily be enriched through genuine communion with God.

Chapter 2

The Explosive Power of Revival

The amazing Christian Revival that came upon the Principality of Wales in 1904 was like a great explosion of spiritual power upon an unsuspecting nation. It had a powerful and life-changing impact upon the people of Wales and many individuals were transformed during those weeks and months of revival. One coal miner talked of having experienced two explosions - the first was when he was working underground in a coal mine and he felt the physical impact of the dust and vibration as the gas explosion took place; the second was the explosion of the Revival when he felt the impact of the presence of God upon his life. He said that the first was as nothing compared with the second! God had a much greater impact than anything that mere nature could produce. The Revival was certainly a significant time in the history of the churches in Wales, as well as in the national life of the Welsh people. In fact, a true understanding of the history of Wales is impossible without an analysis of the impact of the Revival. Unfortunately the 1904 Revival was the last time that the nation as a whole was deeply influenced and powerfully transformed by the great Gospel of our Lord and Saviour Jesus Christ.

The revival started …at Moriah Chapel

The Challenge of Revival

The Revival started in late 1904 at Moriah Chapel in Loughor and the man God used as His instrument in revival was the twenty-six year old Evan Roberts. He was God's chosen vessel to bring Revival to Wales and he became both the voice and the most notable leader in that Revival to the extent that his name will always be associated with the 1904 Welsh Revival. It is a fact that even today most people who know something about the Revival have heard of Evan Roberts yet usually know little or nothing about any other Revival leaders. However, there were other leaders including Rhys Bevan Jones (known as R.B. Jones of the Rhondda), Sydney Evans (who was a former shop assistant and a very close friend of Evan Roberts), Joseph Jenkins, Seth Joshua, D.M. Philips and, in North Wales, J. T Job. All were powerfully and effectively used by God to help bring the Revival message and influence to the whole of Wales.

The Effects of the Revival

The first and most obvious effect was that the churches in Wales were moved out of lethargic complacency and into action. They woke up from their spiritual slumbers, became aware of their sinful condition and began to recognise the vital need to pursue holiness, while prayer and praise started to dominate church services. Repentance, cleansing, confession and forgiveness were the order of the day and there was a wonderful, awe-inspiring awareness of the presence of God. Here was the church opening wide the door and letting in the Saviour, rather than the Saviour on the outside knocking on the door and seeking entry into His church. The Revival started with the spiritual cleansing of many individual Christian lives, along with many churches, where whole congregations were transformed. Truly the words of Peter were experienced: *"For it is a time for judgement to begin with the family of God; and if it begin with us, what will the outcome be for those who do not obey the Gospel of God?"* (1 Peter 4.17). The Welsh Revival,

The Explosive Power of Revival

as with all revivals, began in the churches and therefore amongst the community of Christian believers.

The second great effect is mentioned by Edwin Orr in his book *The Re-study of Revival and Revivalism*. He says that "a hundred thousand outsiders were converted and added to the churches, the vast majority remaining true to the end." This is a staggeringly high figure and when we think of the numbers who were already Christians, the Revival helped to produce a Christianising, indeed even a radical Christianising, of Welsh Society. We can well imagine something of the impact of one hundred thousand new Christians in a small country of a million to a million and half inhabitants. The consequences were certainly very significant in both spiritual and social terms.

So the effect of the Revival upon the church meant a growing desire to preach the Gospel of Jesus Christ and bring the message of salvation to those who were unbelievers. The Revival undoubtedly stirred up a new zeal for evangelism and a deepening concern for those who did not know Christ as their Saviour and Lord. This resulted in the secular world being deeply affected by the Revival as the Gospel radiated out from the churches into the surrounding communities.

Revival certainly stirred up a new zeal for evangelism

The third effect was the tremendous emphasis upon hymn singing and praise to God. "The nightingale of the Revival", Annie Davies, came from my home town of Maesteg. Apparently she regularly gave way to emotion, which would lead her to suddenly and spontaneously burst into song, often cutting across preachers who were giving their ser-

The Challenge of Revival

mons and even causing them, including Evan Roberts, to stop speaking. She was often so overcome with deep feelings and many tears that she could not finish the song, so that both she and the congregation would end up weeping. She frequently sang "the love song of the Revival", *Here is love vast as the ocean.* Her sister Maggie was also used as a singer during the Revival, and there were other notable songsters including Tom Roberts of Towyn, Emlyn Davies of Cefn and Sam Jenkins of Burry Tinplate Works in Llanelli, who was known as "the Sankey of Wales". Much of the singing was in Welsh which gave the congregation a sense of "hwyl". This is basically an emotional quality or feeling inspired as Welsh hymns are sung with deep passion and was a notable feature in congregations moved by the fires of the Revival.

The fourth effect was in the areas of evangelism, mission and preaching. There were significant conversions, as for example, in the town of Maesteg when the Jeffreys brothers, George and Stephen, were converted to Christ in Shiloh Chapel, Nantyffyllon. They went on to conduct huge Gospel and healing campaigns all over Britain and were instrumental in founding the Pentecostal denominations of "Elim" and "Gospel Four Square". They were greatly used by the Lord as they held evangelistic missions across the United Kingdom with huge crowds in attendance. Their graves are to be found just outside Maesteg in the cemetery at Llangynwyd. Sadly the chapel in which they were saved has long been closed and has now been developed into residential units, while keeping the exterior intact.

Pastor Jenkins, was converted when "fire fell" in Cross Hands and he went straight from the "pit to the pulpit", that is, from being a coal miner to being a preacher of the Gospel. Eventually he served the Lord for over twenty years in South Africa. Also John Evans, converted in the Revival, went on to be a medical missionary in India.

The Explosive Power of Revival

It was during the Revival, and in the years immediately following, that many mission halls, Gospel halls and chapels sprang up creating new congregations committed to preaching the Gospel of Jesus Christ. Finally, the influence of the Revival spread to other parts of the United Kingdom and indeed to the four corners of the world. One example in Britain was Charlotte Chapel in Edinburgh where the minister was Joseph Kemp. He witnessed the Revival first hand on a visit to Wales and was deeply impressed and greatly affected by it. On returning to Charlotte Chapel Revival broke out in his own congregation which was consolidated by several Church workers from Wales. It was said at the time that during the Revival it "felt that the fire of God had fallen."

Similarly, after visits to Wales by missionary workers, Revival came to Assam in India, as well as Madagascar which is a large island off the eastern coast of Africa. It was also experienced in Mexico and amongst the congregations of Welsh churches in the United States. In addition there were Revival movements in various European countries such as France, Sweden, Denmark, Germany, Belgium, Hungary and Bulgaria which can be traced back to influences emanating from the Welsh Revival. Also it is clear that Revivals in Africa, Australia, New Zealand, China and Korea were rooted in the 1904 Welsh Revival. Edwin Orr, reflecting on the spread of the Revival from Wales, said, "The story of the Welsh Revival is astounding". So we see that the Welsh Revival acted as a sort of stone in a pond that sends out ripples to all parts of the pond. From the spiritual awakening in a small, insignificant part of the world the ripple effect was felt in the rest of Britain, throughout Europe and into Africa, Asia, Australia and the Americas. The effect of the Welsh Revival was truly global for which we give all the praise and glory to God. The result was that many people were eternally blessed through the work of God's Sovereign Holy Spirit.

The Challenge of Revival

The Welsh Revival was truly global

The fifth effect was upon the social and family lives of the people of Wales. Profound personal and relational changes brought into being different attitudes and reactions which can only be explained in terms of the influence of the Revival. The results of the Revival were major improvements in relationships between people in the community and a greater strength and stability to family life. Thus a greater cohesion and a firmer foundation came into Welsh life, as the following make clear.

    a. **Drunkenness:** Convictions for drunkenness fell dramatically. In Glamorgan there were 10,528 convictions for drunkenness in 1903 but this figure had fallen to 5,490 in 1906. So the numbers were almost halved in the most populous county in Wales. The Chief Constable of Glamorgan wrote in March 1905, "The decrease in drunkenness has undoubtedly been most marked where the Revivalists have had the largest following." One police sergeant commented to the visiting Bishop of Dorking, "There are twenty-two licensed houses in my district and they are not drawing enough beer to pay the gas, the men are all in the chapels." It must have been a rich blessing to many families that the man of the house came home with his wages rather than having spent that money on drink, not to mention less drink-induced violence and argument. Clearly family life became more stable, less divisive and much more harmonious. The effects upon the children must have been powerfully positive.

The Explosive Power of Revival

b. **Restitution:** It was found that the Revival caused many people to have a tender conscience about unpaid debts. It must have come as a pleasant, if unexpected, surprise to numerous shopkeepers when they found people coming to pay their debts, even debts that had long been written off. So even in the commercial world the influence of the Revival was felt. This has been dubbed the "economics of revival". A reduction in stealing from work was another consequence and this coupled with less drunkenness, would have meant a much more stable and able work force for the many employers in Wales. It would also have greatly eased the pressures upon the forces of law and order.

The economics of revival

c. **Unity:** In church life it was noted that the Revival reduced, and even removed, sectionalism and suspicion. Rhys Jones commented that "denominational walls, as high perhaps in Wales as in most countries, fell down as did Jericho's walls." Both Anglican and non-conformist ministers came together in a wonderful wholeness, an evangelical unity and oneness. Thus the ongoing emphasis was much less on what divided Christians, those secondary issues that can loom so large in the minds of many people of God. Instead, the focus of attention was upon the major doctrines of the faith that all Christian believers hold, namely the deity of Christ, the Trinity, the work of atonement, the need for justification by faith and the reality of judgement. The primary truths of oneness in the body of Christ became much more important to God's people.

The Challenge of Revival

d. **Family life:** One NSPCC inspector saw such a remarkable change in families touched by the Revival that he no longer needed to watch several such families whom he had previously expected to prosecute for neglect of their children. Thus parents touched by God through the Revival became attentive to the needs of their offspring and family life became much more important to them. At the other end of the age spectrum, it was reported that a number of families in Swansea were removing aged parents from the workhouses to care for them at home. Revival certainly had an enriching effect upon family life.

Revival had an enriching effect upon family life

e. **Bad language and swearing:** People's ways of speaking became more wholesome and gentler. Cursing, swearing and blasphemy were greatly reduced and this was seen everywhere including the workplaces where tough men earned their living such as the coal mines and the steelworks. We have all heard of the "pit ponies unused to the new kindness and clean language, without the usual kicks and curses, who almost stopped work until they got adjusted." (Whitaker) It is amazing to think that Revival also affected the animals and those pit ponies so used to being physically abused with kicks and verbally abused with bad language, initially being unable to understand the new kindliness that revival had brought to those coal miners. It is recorded that miners would go early to their shifts so that they could spend time together in prayer and Bible reading. One colliery even had its own chapel underground which was cut into the coal bearing rock and had

The Explosive Power of Revival

crude seating made from the rock seams themselves. Certainly the atmosphere at the various workplaces was greatly improved as a result of the Revival.

It was reported that whole football and rugby teams were converted to Christ during the Revival and that fixtures had to be abandoned because team members were more interested in praying than playing. This is not to say that playing sports is wrong; it is just that the players became more interested in worshipping God than competing on the field of play.

One further interesting aspect of the Revival was that it deeply touched children. It is said that many children met for prayer, even using the school playground for the purpose as well as barns and empty pigsties. The North Wales Guardian for 27th January 1905 referred to a "Sunday afternoon children's prayer meeting", followed by youngsters conducting a short service in the public square.

Thus the work and the effects of the Revival in Wales in 1904 were extensive affecting all age groups and both male and female. It affected visitors to the Principality as well as local people. It changed the character of many individuals, many families, many churches and many places of employment. Indeed the whole community was affected. Also its influence spread far and wide across the country of Britain and on to the ends of the earth. To summarise: "The difficulty used to be to get the people into the church, but the difficulty now is to get them out of it!" Our prayer is that we would once again see such wonderful blessings in our country again.

Chapter 3

The Rise and Fall of the Revival

As we have seen the Welsh Revival of 1904 was a most remarkable movement of the Spirit of God. It transformed the spiritual, cultural and social landscape of the Principality. Family life was radically improved for those who were influenced by the Revival. Churches were revitalised and became dynamic in their proclamation of the Gospel. Indeed it is reported that there were one hundred thousand converts to Christ during the time of Revival and this had a very big impact upon such a small nation. The man whose name is known above all others as the one used by God to bring about the Revival was Evan Roberts. He saw a mighty anointing of God's Spirit, time and again, upon many congregations throughout the South Wales industrial valleys. He had been prepared by God for the wonderful work of being at the centre of the great Revival in Wales. Yet he was not the only reason for the Revival.

Why did Revival come to Wales in 1904?

Ultimately, revival is the sovereign and mysterious work of God but He uses human means as part of His great plan. Let us consider two factors.

The Challenge of Revival

People

Brian Edwards wrote in his book *Revival*, "Revival commences with those who in bad times remain good, in godless days remain Christian, in careless years remain constant and who have eternity in their hearts." Thus, in Revival times, God uses those individuals who are spiritually prepared, who are able to be sensitive to God's Spirit and are aware of His work. This certainly seems to have been true of Evan Roberts in Wales. Evan Roberts and others like him were desperate for holiness, being utterly dissatisfied with worldliness, materialism and shallowness. These were people who searched for God with all their hearts and had deep personal relationships with the Lord. In the words of one commentator, they "fear God and sin and nothing else". Of Evan Roberts it was said that "above all he is faithful to God and his conscience; he cannot be bought or bribed; his strength is his character sanctified by communion with the invisible". (Pritchard) Are we willing to pay such a price for Revival? Will we ever be God's channels for Revival to our generation? If so we also must be utterly devoted to the Lord.

Fear God and sin and nothing else

Prayer

No revival has ever been witnessed that did not start with people committed to prayer. For example, the Ulster Revival of 1859 can be traced to a group of young converts who were committed to "the secret of holy supplication". The prayer that brings revival is urgent, bold

The Rise and Fall of the Revival

and continuous, as Brian Edwards writes: "They are never flippant and careless before God, nor are they over familiar or presumptuous; but they are bold." This was seen in Wales prior to the great events of the Revival as the following two specific examples make clear.

   a. In 1904 Joseph Jenkins in Cardiganshire was deeply concerned for the young people in his church. They were careless about spiritual matters and so he decided to spend time praying for them. His burden was so great that he was known to lose all sense of time as he prayed for the spiritual welfare of those young people.

   b. From 1897, a group of young ministers met together to pray for Revival. "This fellowship intensified their hunger, bringing it at last to a pitch near to desperation". (R.B. Jones)

Undoubtedly there were others who were engaged in urgent and vital prayer to God for revival in Wales. Such prayer is never self-centred but for the glory of God and the blessing of others. Indeed, when God's people are so burdened that they pray with such deep earnestness then it might well be the sign that Revival is coming. Matthew Henry wrote, "When God intends great mercy for his people, the first thing he does is to set them a-praying."

The secret of holy supplication

James Alexander Stewart wrote the following in his book *Revival and You*: "I knew a local church in an Eastern European land which, because of coldness, had only twenty believers gathering on Sunday night for Bible study. Some suggested that they close the building and

The Challenge of Revival

give up their testimony in that…city. A few held on in faith and, with careful dedication, being elderly people, had a solemn meeting of dedication where they told God that whatever should be the price for an awakening in their church and city they were willing to pay it…They continued for many months seeking the face of the Lord…They would not let go of the Lord until He had blessed them. When I began meetings in their church, many hundreds of souls were saved from the opening nights, many among them being the children of those who had been praying. So mightily did the Lord work in the church to the salvation of souls that very soon the building, which seated eight hundred people, was packed to capacity at every meeting. Without pastor, they soon overflowed their banks, so that some twenty mission stations were established…The deadest church in the nation became the most spiritual and wide awake." It is a very moving and challenging account and highlights the sacrifice that we have to be willing to make if we are ever going see Revival touch our nation again.

So we see two aspects to revival which God uses; the right people and right prayers. The two go very much together and have the effect of moving the hand of God so that His Holy Spirit descends in mighty anointed power. Indeed the apostle James wrote in the New Testament, ***"The prayer of a righteous man is powerful and effective."*** (James 5.16) So we have some insight into why the Welsh Revival came in 1904. We now need to ask another question, which is of vital importance, and that is: "Why the Revival died out and disappeared?"

Why Did the Welsh Revival Fizzle Out?

One of the saddest aspects of the 1904 Welsh Revival was that one fifth of the converts to Christ fell away from their commitment to church life. However, that still leaves eighty thousand who remained faithful to the Lord and to His Word. Yet it is also true that within ten

The Rise and Fall of the Revival

years the fires of revival had died out and the wonder of that great outpouring was simply an increasingly distant memory. The reasons for this decline are complex and tangled but we will look at some of the strands and hopefully learn lessons for our own spiritual development. We must heed the warnings if we are to avoid walking along the same downward track in our own personal lives. So why did the fires of revival die out so quickly?

1. We need to take a look at the revivalist, Evan Roberts, himself. Something strange happened to this man, which may have adversely affected the Revival. He had some kind of breakdown and went to live in Leicester in the home of Mr and Mrs Penn-Lewis. There, he became a recluse and utterly refused to see visitors, including family and friends. No one was allowed to see him and every attempt was frustrated as he adamantly turned away all who came to the house to visit him. Such behaviour led to many rumours being circulated about him and they in turn had a negative affect upon the Revival. Evan Roberts lived for many years after the Revival and eventually died in Cardiff in 1951.

2. "Modernism" and liberal preaching were instrumental in nullifying the work of the Revival. Those liberal teachers preached against the Bible as the Word of God and Jesus as the eternal Son of God. Someone has written that "modernism took the pulpit and emptied the chapels." Certainly such an approach to Christian ministry had the effect of destroying the dynamic of the Gospel.

"modernism took the pulpit and emptied the chapels"

The Challenge of Revival

3. The impact of the First World War, which came within ten years of the Revival, helped to undermine its potency. Many young men who were converted during the Welsh Revival found themselves choking and dying in the mud and the gas of the Great War battlefields of France. It heralded the death of the youthful flower of the Revival. Many died, while others were wounded and many came back broken and disillusioned. A potentially powerful generation of leaders was lost. Indeed a generation became lost to the cause of Christianity in Wales and many churches never really recovered.

4. The fourth factor is one we need to explore with a measure of care as it can be very sensitive to some people. One writer has said that "Welsh nationalism sealed the death of the Revival". Essentially, because English had become the language spoken by the majority of the people of Wales, with fewer and fewer being brought up speaking Welsh it was feared by some Welsh speakers that the language would die out and in the 1960s it certainly did seem as though it would become a dead language. Many chapel leaders started to focus more upon the Welsh language, culture and national identity and too often this became more important to them than the Gospel. I know of one chapel in an area where the vast majority of people spoke English and which had over thirty children in the Sunday School. A new minister took over and insisted that all services, including Sunday School, be conducted in Welsh and before long all the children left because they couldn't speak Welsh and had no idea what was going on in the services. That Chapel has stood derelict for many years and is a powerful reminder that the Gospel must be the main priority of the spiritual life in the congregation of any Chapel.

The Rise and Fall of the Revival

Failure to insist that the Gospel be the main priority

5. The Revival produced a great deal of emotion as people became convicted by their sins and cried out to God for mercy and salvation. Unfortunately there were those who focused more upon the supposed manifestations of the Spirit than upon God. All sorts of extreme behaviour were witnessed - swooning, hysteria, commotion, noise, disorder, dreams, tongues and visions. Hard on the heels of the Revival came these displays of somewhat strange and unusual behaviour in many congregations. It was all too easy to become consumed with the spectacle of those outlandish happenings and to lose sight of the holiness of Almighty God. Evan Roberts was so concerned not to meddle with the work of the Spirit that he allowed meetings largely to run themselves, which had the effect of encouraging excessive emotional behaviour and many people think that such conduct helped to kill the Revival.

6. The Welsh Revival was not consolidated as fully as it could have been because it was not always accompanied by sound Bible teaching. It is true that many people did revere the Bible as a result of the Revival and I well remember as a teenager meeting a lady who was converted in the Welsh Revival and had learnt many passages of the Bible off by heart. It was amazing to hear that she had memorised not only the whole of the New Testament but the whole of the first five books of the Bible and also all of the Psalms. Maybe she had a photographic memory but I was, to say the least, deeply impressed. However, such a reverence and devotion

The Challenge of Revival

to the Word of God may not have been universal in all Welsh chapel circles.

Someone has written: "Every experience and teaching in revival must be checked by 'what is written' and every deviation from this should be clearly corrected.". This was undoubtedly lacking in many areas where the Revival took hold. This particular failure was so glaring that it was probably the main reason why so many converts seem to have fallen away in the few years following the 1904 Revival. More fell away than for any other Revival for which we have records. Evan Roberts neglected preaching in his Revival meetings as he was too overly conscious that he must not interfere with the working of the Holy Spirit. The Bible was not really given its rightful place and so the problems mentioned ensued. People presumably thought that in some way the Spirit and the Bible were incompatible.

It has been said that "the centrality of Bible preaching is a sound curb to excess and error and is, after all, one thing God has clearly committed to his church." It is strange that Evan Roberts himself did not see this and unfortunately such neglect removed from Wales many of the ongoing benefits that could have continued to flow from the Revival.

7. There was overt opposition to the Revival and severe criticism of the Revival leaders both in verbal and written forms. Evan Roberts was denounced publicly by some people and even by preachers who had seen their own congregations richly blessed and increased as a result of the Revival. Some people called him dangerous, while others mocked and jeered at him. It is certainly true that every work of God has been criticised and opposed and so this must not be considered unusual. However it was undoubtedly another factor that led to the slowing down and eventual demise of the 1904 Welsh Revival.

The Rise and Fall of the Revival

It is awe inspiring to recall what God did in so many lives in the Principality of Wales a hundred years ago. The accomplishments were great and we rejoice that there was such a wonderful expansion of God's church in the nation. Yet we are saddened that it died out so quickly and that today there is very little evidence of that great outpouring of blessing through the wonderful power of the Holy Spirit. We must take up the challenge to pray for Revival in our own hearts and in our particular church. The price will be high if we truly mean business with God and will entail giving ourselves to God in committed and devoted prayer. We must determine every day to draw close to God and continue to hold on to Him with the prayer of faith until He rains down the mighty blessings of another Revival. Yet prayer is so much more than simply saying words. It is drawing close to God with pure and righteous lives. It is letting the cleansing work of Christ's shed blood and the washing of the pure Word of God take place in our lives and then the God of holiness can truly answer our prayers.

Prayer is much more than simply words

Revival always begins with committed Christians devoting themselves to prayer. God, in a mysterious way, is moved to respond to the prayers of His people and we must believe that one day He will again rain down the mighty fire of Revival upon our nation. It will be a time when the whole community will lift up its voice and once again sing "Dyma gariad fel y moroedd", that great hymn of William Rees, "Here is love vast as the ocean"..

Chapter 4

The Conditions for Revival
(2 Chronicles 7.14)

In 1835 Titus Coan landed on one of the islands of Hawaii in the Pacific Ocean and set about doing evangelistic work, by proclaiming the Gospel of Jesus Christ to the islanders. It is recorded that in 1837 "the fires of revival broke" and there was a very great and powerful anointing by God's Holy Spirit upon the inhabitants. Many people were saved and as a result their lives were transformed. Quarrels, sometimes of long standing, were made up and relationships were healed. Hopeless drunkards were reclaimed and went on to live lives of sober delight. Adulterers were saved and they became faithful to their spouses. Thieves returned property that they had stolen. The whole community was transformed and deeply influenced for good by that great revival. In one year 5,244 people joined the church and on one memorable Sunday, 1,705 new Christians were baptised. Such figures stagger us as we can hardly comprehend them. Yet they remind us of the beginning, the birthday of the church, when 3,000 precious souls were converted to Christ following Peter's sermon on the Day of Pentecost (Acts 2). Certainly that work in Hawaii was a great and mighty moving of God's Spirit and many people were so changed that they were never the same again.

'the fires of revival broke'

The Challenge of Revival

There are similar experiences in all revivals such as in the "Great Awakening" in America during the time of Jonathan Edwards. In Britain, there was the great Methodist Revival under the anointed preaching of John Wesley and George Whitefield, which saved Britain from a blood bath such as engulfed France during its Revolution. In Wales, there were the Revivals of 1859 under David Morgan's ministry and, of course, 1904 with Evan Roberts. In 1859, there was the Ulster Revival, while in 1947 Duncan Campbell witnessed the outpouring of God's Spirit in the Outer Hebrides. There have been Revivals in many parts of the world and in many periods of history. Always, the effect has been deeply beneficial to the community and the influence has always been for good.

We wonder whether we will ever see anything similar in Wales or anywhere else in Britain again. Indeed, could the Western world ever again feel the effects of spiritual revival such as have been described here? Some of us may answer with a resounding "No" because we could never envisage churches full to overflowing and a spiritual impact being made with the Gospel on the community at large.

The Western world is currently dominated by the ideologies of secularism, atheism, post-modernism and hedonism. All these ideas exclude God in one form or another and focus exclusively upon the selfish desires of man. Secularism sees God as excluded from a public role in local or national affairs and from important decisions in the life and leadership of the community. There is horror and outrage if a leader suggests the need to pray and therefore to consult God about the issues of the day. Atheism makes no pretence and totally excludes God from all parts of life, claiming that He does not exist. Post modernism takes away one of the great pillars of Christianity and that is the rock solid foundation of historical fact and evidence, upon which Christianity is based. Essentially, post modernists deny the validity of evidence, sug-

The Conditions for Revival

gesting that evidence only appears as evidence to the one who is convinced of its veracity. Thus they deny objective truth. Hedonism is the idea of "eat, drink and be merry". It is rampant consumerism and with people in the Western world having more free time and more disposable income than ever before, this ideology has already become a way of life.

Is it possible that into this mix the Lord could send His Holy Spirit? Some have concluded that it is impossible and that now we are very near the end of the present age. Thus they feel that we should simply wait for the return of our Saviour from Heaven and mark time until we enter the glory of God's eternal presence. It is even said that now we live in "the day of small things" and we should not expect another awakening from the Lord. Indeed one church leader was heard to say that he didn't want outsiders to come into his church as they would only bring problems. Effectively, he could already write the word "closed" above the front door of his church building. It is all too easy to lose our vision of the greatness of God when we feel overwhelmed and inundated with the influence of worldliness, immorality and what we feel are declining standards within our society and amongst those with whom we come in contact.

Revival always begins with the church

Yet we must remember that Revival always begins with the church – with those people who have been saved through the shed blood of Christ. We must not allow ourselves ever to become content with shallowness, spiritual mediocrity, a weak understanding of Scripture or a soul that is starved of true spiritual nourishment. We must be prepared to pay the price for Revival and if we never see another national awakening we should at least see Revival in our own lives on a daily basis.

The Challenge of Revival

Yet so often we are afraid of such a move by God in our lives and we do not want to be disturbed out of our comfortable lifestyle. We don't want to concentrate on prayer and preaching. We don't really want anything to change the way we do things in our churches and certainly don't want the pattern of our worship structures to be tampered with in any way. What would our reaction be if someone cried out in one of our church services, "What must I do to be saved?" Assuming it was not simply a stunt; it would undoubtedly be a cry from deep within the soul of someone disturbed by sin, but would our reaction be one of shock and disbelief or would it be to rejoice that the Lord was working in someone's life by His Holy Spirit?

It has to be said that, in the Western world generally, the church is finding the going tough and difficult. The preaching of the Gospel is hardly finding much of a response and the lasting fruit of people being saved is very limited. It is a time of discouragement, closure and decline. Yet, as we read the words of God in 2 Chronicles 7.14, we find that this was exactly the type of situation that the Lord was addressing. We read, "*If my people, which are called by my name, shall humble themselves, and pray, and seek my face, and turn from their wicked ways; then will I hear from heaven, and will forgive their sin, and will heal their land.*" For Israel, at that time, heaven was shut up and there was no refreshing rain. The good things had been replaced by bad things. Doesn't that almost sounds like a description of our age when there seems to be no blessing from Heaven? It is as if Heaven were silent. We see past blessings rapidly eroding and disappearing. Then God says, "*if my people, who are called by my name*", and this is clearly a reference to the Old Testament people of God who were the citizens of the nation of Israel.

However in the New Testament the people of God do not take the name of Israel but are identified with Christ. So, Revival must begin

The Conditions for Revival

with Christians - those who are called by the name of the Saviour, who are spiritually alive in Christ. Clearly, Revival can have no effect upon those who are spiritually dead. The dead cannot be revived but even the weakest Christian and the weakest church can be revived. Indeed D.M. Paton described Revival as "the inrush of God's Spirit into a body which threatens to become a corpse!" Surely the church in the West is very nearly a corpse but there still beats the faint pulse of spiritual life and so God can revive it.

Vance Havner wrote: "Revival is God rending the heavens and coming down upon His people." We need reviving; we need a fresh anointing of God's Spirit; we need that dynamic of Christian living that only the Holy Spirit can engender in us. Yet there is a price; there is a cost. Are we willing to pay it? Alan Redpath wrote: "There is no Revival possible in any fellowship without a price being paid."

We need reviving

In 2 Chronicles 7.14 the Lord outlines the price that needs to be paid by giving four important principles for revival.

1. We must be Humble

So the Lord says, "*If my people, who are called by my name, will humble themselves...*" and thus it is obvious that pride hinders revival, while humility helps to engender it.

The late Oswald J. Smith wrote a book entitled, *The Revival We Need* and which was later republished under the title, *Hunger for Revival*. In one of the chapters he outlines twenty-four obstacles to Revival, one of

The Challenge of Revival

which is pride. He wrote: "Is there any pride in our hearts? Are we puffed up? Do we think a great deal of our own position and attainments? This prevents the work of God in our midst and is called sin – we need to forsake and confess it." Also the late Christian communicator Arthur Skevington Wood wrote, "The greatest hindrance to Revival is pride amongst the Lord's people."

Pride is always a danger and can raise its head in our lives all too easily. Pride can be seen in our criticism of others, in our anger towards people, in our gossip about others, in our jealous reactions, in our belief in the rightness of everything we say and our condemnation of the ideas of others. It can also be seen in the harsh, hard judgemental attitude we display and in our bitter hearts when we don't get our own way. It can be seen in our desire for prominence, for leadership and our unwillingness to do the menial and seemingly trivial matters that are so important in a local church. It can also be seen in our unwillingness to go the extra mile in caring and showing compassion towards others.

Pride is always a danger

It is all too easy to glory in our education and academic qualifications, in our position and status or in our earning capacity and material possessions. How shallow all these things are in the light of eternity! We should glory in Christ alone and in His atoning work on the cross of Calvary and thus learn the true meaning of humility.

When the Apostle Paul wrote from prison to the Philippians one of the factors he brought out was the need for humility. So he wrote, "***Do nothing out of selfish ambition or vain conceit, but in humility consider others better than yourselves.***" (2.3). He then went on in chap-

The Conditions for Revival

ter two to give four illustrations of people who had the heart of humility.

i. Christ (v.6-8)

The blessed Saviour, our Lord Jesus Christ, was and is God the Son. He is co-equal with the Father and yet He was willing to divest Himself of the glory and majesty of being God and came and indwelt a human body. The Creator confined Himself to the physical weaknesses and limitations of that human body. That is great condescension and yet His humility went much further than that because He allowed death to have its hold upon Him. It is incredible to think that the Lord of life and glory submitted Himself to death. He said that no one could take His life from Him and that He had power to lay it down and power to take it again. Charles Wesley, in one of his hymns, highlighted the wonder of it when he wrote, "Tis mystery all the immortal dies." Essentially, he wrote of a seeming contradiction because immortality by its very nature does not die. Mortality, not immortality, is subject to death. Yet our Saviour died not just any sort of death but the death of crucifixion, which is a death of unimaginable pain and shame. To the Jews it was a curse to be hung on a cross but He took our curse and through Him we can be free from the curse of our sins and enjoy the wonder of forgiveness and eternal life.

The stoop of Christ, from Heaven's highest glory to Calvary's depth of woe, demonstrates the greatness of the humility of our Lord. Yet such an example might have seemed too great for the Philippians and so Paul gave a second example of true humility.

ii. Paul (v.17)

In an oblique way, the apostle introduced himself and demonstrated that he too was willing to die for the sake of the Philippians. He was humble enough to give for the sake of other people. He saw himself as a drink offering that was poured, in Old Testament times, upon the main sacrifice on the altar. He writes, "***But even I am being poured like a drink offering on the sacrifice...***". Thus Paul demonstrated the mind of Christ, which was the sacrificial giving of self for the sake of others. Yet there may have been some at Philippi who would have felt that this was the normal, expected attitude to be demonstrated in an apostle and as they were not apostles how could they live like that. So Paul gives a third example of true humility.

iii. Timothy (v.19-24)

This time Paul's younger missionary colleague was used as an example of having the mind of Christ. Timothy took a genuine interest in other people, neglecting his own needs to help meet the needs of others. He was an outstanding servant of Jesus Christ. However we can again imagine those who might think that Timothy, as a missionary, would be expected to live this sort of life. So Paul, as if listening to those thoughts, gives a fourth and final example of true humility.

iv. Epaphroditus (v.25-30)

Epaphroditus was not an apostle nor a missionary, but simply one of the leaders of the church at Philippi. He showed this tremendous humility by quietly and sacrificially serving the needs of other people. Epaphroditus truly reflected the heart of humility and therefore walked in the footsteps of His Saviour. Could we be added to this list of people who walked in humbleness before their God? Humbleness is certainly a vital need if we are ever to see Revival again in our land.

The Conditions for Revival

Humbleness is certainly a vital need

Yet if personal pride is a problem, so too is denominational pride – the feeling that we, as a group, are right and everyone else is somehow defective in their understanding and application of Scripture. We must be careful not to disparage other groups of the Lord's people simply because they do not see everything in the same light as we do. If they hold to the core truths of the Christian faith, then they are our brothers and sisters in Christ, and so there should be no sense in which we deal with them as from a superior position, as we are all one in the body of Christ. If there is pride in our hearts then now is the time to confess and renounce it before God with true repentance.

Humility is not the same thing as an inferiority complex. We are not called to feel inferior but we are called to be humble. The inferior person feels so inadequate and worthless that he does nothing for God. The humble person feels inadequate but is willing to do whatever God asks of him, knowing that he could never accomplish anything apart from the resources that the Lord supplies. May we never be complacent but continually seek the Lord's presence and power in our lives as we approach Him with reverent humility and desire only His glory in Revival.

So the first requirement that the Lord demands of His people is humbleness.

2. We Must Be Prayerful

The Lord says, "*If my people, who are called by my name, will humble themselves and pray...*", and clearly this applies in two direc-

The Challenge of Revival

tions. There is need for personal prayer and there is need for corporate prayer. It is said that on the Saturday night before C. H. Spurgeon took up what was to become a Spirit-anointed ministry in London, a group of people met in the basement of a church in Newport, South Wales to pray. They prayed specifically for the Lord to bless richly the ministry of Spurgeon. They kept that Saturday evening prayer meeting going for thirty years; few of the group died or left during that time and their prayers were abundantly answered, as God brought almost continuous Revival to London during Spurgeon's years of preaching the Gospel. It is reported that every Sunday he preached directly to crowds of up to 10,000 people and each week his sermons sold up to 30,000 copies. It was a great time as God anointed the preaching of the Word through Spurgeon and many people were saved as a result.

Prayer is vitally important in the work of God. Leonard Ravenhill wrote, "The church is dying on its feet because it is not living on its knees." Someone else wrote that, "the prayer meeting is Biblical, historical, educational, vital, instrumental and fundamental because it gives birth to revolutionaries and is the making of an unstoppable force." The 1859 Ulster Revival, which saw 100,000 people converted to Christ, started with three people believing and practicing "the secret of holy supplication". In 1739, David Brainard, a young man in his twenties, wrestled all night in prayer with God and longed for blessing upon the Native American Indians of the Eastern United States. Subsequently, the Spirit of God moved in mighty power as Revival broke out amongst those Indians and many were drawn to Christ. Brownlow North wrote over one hundred years ago in words that ring true today, "I believe there is one thing for which God is very angry with our land and for which His Holy Spirit is so little seen among us, that is the neglect of united prayer, the appointed means of bringing down the Holy Spirit."

The Conditions for Revival

"the church is dying on its feet because it is not living on its knees"

What is prayer? It is a heart that yearns for God and will not let go of God until He bestows the blessing. It is, therefore, much more than simply saying words and if it is only words then surely it isn't prayer. It is being in contact with the living God and anything in our lives that weakens that contact must be removed and renounced. Every sin must be removed as well as every kind of selfishness, every aspect of unbelief and anything doubtful. Instead we must focus with total devotion upon the Lord.

So, when we pray, we must remember the following.

a. **Personal righteousness.** Our prayers must flow from a life that is lived in holy obedience to the commands of the Lord. Sinning and praying do not go together. Our prayers will not be truly answered unless we confess and renounce our sinfulness.

b. **A heart of forgiveness.** In Mark 11.25 Jesus indicates very clearly that if our prayers are to be effective then we must be willing to forgive others. He says, *"**when you stand praying forgive**"*. Obviously it is impossible to commune with the God of forgiveness if we are unwilling to be forgiving.

c. **Unity with fellow believers.** It is clear that true blessing and Christian unity go together and this was certainly true of the early church, as recorded in the opening chapters of Acts. Also, Psalm 133 mentions that the place where God chooses to bestow His blessing is in the place of unity amongst His people.

The Challenge of Revival

    d. **Seek no personal glory.** Any sense of prominence for self-glory nullifies the work of prayer and withholds the blessing of the Lord.

    e. **Seek the God of glory and the glory of God.** This must always be the focus of our prayers. We must desire the Lord and seek to glorify His name in all our actions and in all our words.

We need very much to get back to serious prayer times where Christians meet together for true intercession before the Lord. This may require us to sacrifice such things as sleep or food in order to find time to pray. Yet it is vital if we are ever to witness another visitation of the Lord in mighty Revival blessing. Are we prepared to bring ourselves constantly into close contact with the Lord and listen to His voice, as we battle through in prayer until the victory is achieved? Someone has written, "until we know the brokenness of prayer, we will never know the blessing of prayer." May we be people who practice the reality of prayer and experience its power.

'until we know the brokenness of prayer, we will never know the blessing of prayer'

---

3. We must seek His Face

The Lord says, "*If my people, who are called by my name, will humble themselves and pray and seek my face…*" So we need to seek the face of God if we are ever to experience Revival.

Someone has written: "When God tells his people to seek His face, He

The Conditions for Revival

is urging them to live in such a way that his face can be turned in their direction. They can enjoy the smile of the Lord because they are living in the centre of His will." So, the revived Christian is the one living in the will of God and doing what the Lord desires through obedience and surrender.

Yet, how can we live in the centre of the will of God? The answer is by focusing upon the Word of God. God will not trust revival to those who will not trust His Word. The Bible must be of primary importance in our lives because it is the revelation of God to mankind. There is no other message that is divinely given and Revival does not break out amongst those who reject the Bible's inspiration and inerrancy. Revival comes to those who love the Word of God, who know the Word of God, who study the Word of God, who preach the Word of God and who are willing to obey the Word of God.

I once listened to a minister of a church which had seen phenomenal growth. They had outgrown their building and had developed larger premises and still they were at bursting point as far as the capacity of the church building was concerned. Yet that minister said, "I have only one commission from God and that is to teach the Bible, nothing else!" It was a startling reminder that we do not need gimmicks or imitations of worldly ways. It is the Bible alone that is God's essential message to mankind, though it does need to be taught to the people in a clear, compelling and relevant manner.

Errol Hulse said that "an indispensable sign of true Revival is that the Word of God grows mightily and prevails – it spreads widely and grows in power." Also Arthur Skevington Wood wrote that "it may be said that Revivals thrive on the Word and the Word is exalted in Revivals."

The Challenge of Revival

"revivals thrive on the Word"

The Word leads us to an understanding of the mind and heart of God. We learn what pleases our Saviour and we learn the pathway to obedience and these are vitally important preliminaries to seeking His face. We can only seek the face of God if we are prepared to alter our lives to please the Saviour and be totally under the Lordship of Jesus Christ. May we experience the smiling countenance of our God upon us and may we have the joy and delight of experiencing an outpouring of God's Spirit in our times.

4. We Must Turn From Our Wicked Ways

The Lord says, ***"If my people, who are called by my name, will humble themselves and pray and seek my face and turn from their wicked ways..."*** So we need to turn from our wicked ways if we are ever to see Revival.

The whole idea of turning from sin is summarised in the word repentance. True repentance in the hearts of God's praying people leads to the blessing of further repentance during times of Revival. Indeed one of the glories of Revival is the desire to turn from sin in repentance and pursue the Lord in holiness. Errol Hulse wrote, "The chief authentic mark of Revival is enduring repentance."

The mighty preacher John Wesley wrote in 1734: "My one aim in life is to secure personal holiness, for without being holy myself I cannot promote real holiness in others." From the pen of Brian Edwards we have: "Together with our prayerlessness, it is probably the unholiness of the lives of Christian leaders today that convinces God we are not

The Conditions for Revival

really serious about Revival."

There is a desperate need for a burden to be laid upon us, a burden to repent. It is imperative that we turn from and renounce not just the fruit of sin but also its root. The fruit are the sins we commit - lust, gossip, intemperate remarks, foul language and so on. The root goes to the very heart of our lives and essentially is about control. Who is at the controls of my life? Is it me or is it Christ? It is in the inscrutable parts of my life that I must truly repent and seek the Lord's forgiveness. It is in those secret areas that are hidden from the eyes of other people, where cherished sins lurk - rooms in my life where the Lord has no entry, centres of darkness and self-indulgence. It is in these areas that we must truly repent if we are ever to see revival again in our land.

a burden to repent

Are we ready to give rather than to get, to sacrifice rather than be self-indulgent? If the answer is 'No' then we need to search our hearts before God and come to the point of sincere repentance, to the place where we are willing to obey the Lord and turn away from all wickedness and sin.

So we find the conditions that the Lord laid down for His people to experience revival in this vital Old Testament verse. We are called to humble ourselves, pray, seek God through His Word and repent of sin by walking in holiness. This is the abiding challenge for us today. If we fulfil these conditions, then this verse goes on to say that there will be a threefold result.

1. **God will hear from Heaven.** The Lord, of course, hears ev-

The Challenge of Revival

erything that is said and knows all things. However the implication in this verse is that the Lord hears and answers the prayers of His people. Thus when the conditions are met, God promises to hear the cries of His people. So, if our prayers are not being answered at the moment then we should search our hearts and lives to see if anything that grieves the Lord is present which therefore should be removed.

2. **God will forgive their sin.** This is a wonderful blessing to know that our sins are forgiven. It is a relief to be assured that we no longer have the burden of sin resting upon us. Certainly, during Revival times, people have experienced the vivid reality of their sin and have cried out to God for deliverance and mercy. The subsequent blessing of salvation and eternal life has been a great joy and delight in the knowledge of forgiveness.

3. **God will heal their land.** This particularly applied to Israel, with its agricultural dependence. The land would return to real fertility when the people of the nation truly repented and did what God wanted them to do. In our own land it is much more likely that the emphasis is upon the healing of relationships in families, marriages, churches, the work place and the community at large. That is moral healing and the restoration of tranquillity and contentment instead of disturbance, fear and worry being the order of the day.

The Lord promises very rich and great blessings to His people when they are willing to fulfil His conditions for Revival. We pray that we might once again experience in our land the fires of revival falling upon individuals and transforming them. We pray that we might see those fires falling upon churches and changing them. We look forward

The Conditions for Revival

to the fires of God's Revival falling upon our nation and transforming the people into a community in whom God takes delight.

Let our prayer be in the words of this hymn by Albert Midlane.

> 'Revive your work, O Lord,
> Your mighty arm make bare.
> Speak with the voice that wakes the dead,
> And make your people hear!'

Again as we pray for Revival we can also use the words of another hymn,

> 'Send a revival, start the work in me.
> See if there be some wicked way in me.
> Cleanse me from every sin and set me free.'

God calls us to pray for Revival, to expect Revival and to look for Revival. Yet even if there is no national outpouring of God's Spirit we should live every day in personal Revival. May that be our rich blessing day by day as we serve the Saviour and live in obedience for His glory.

Further Reading

"*A Diary of Revival*" by Kevin Adams (Crusade for World Revival)

"*A Pictorial History of Revival*" by Kevin Adams & Emyr Jones (Crusade for World Revival)

"*Voices from the Welsh Revival*" by Brynmor P. Jones (Evangelical Press of Wales)

"*Revival*" by Brian H. Edwards (Evangelical Press)

"*Great Revivals*" by Colin Whittaker (Marshalls)

"*Revival and You*" by James Alexander Stewart (Revival Literature)

"*Revival*" by Richard Owen Roberts (Richard Owen Roberts, Publishers)

"*I saw the Welsh Revival*" by David Matthews (Ambassador)

"*What is Revival?*" by G.J. Morgan (Ambassador)

"*Lord, Open the Heavens*" by Stephen F. Olford (Harold Shaw Publishers)

"*Out of the Rut, into Revival*" by A.W. Tozer (Hodder & Stoughton)

"*The "Fifty Nine" Revival*" by Ian R.K. Paisley (Martyrs Memorial Free Presbyterian Church)

"*The Price and Power of Revival*" by Duncan Campbell (Parry Jackman)

"*Revival Comes to Wales*" by Eifion Evans (Evangelical Press of Wales)

"*The Revival we Need*" by Oswald J. Smith (Marshall, Morgan and Scott Ltd)

Books by Paul Young

'The End of a Nation'
(Studies in Obadiah) (£2.00)

'The Friend and Promise of God'
(Abraham & Isaac) (£2.50)

'Understanding the Bible'
(Inspiration, Inerrancy & Interpretation) (£4.00)

'Outreach Through the Local Church'
(Problems & Needs) (£1.50)

'Understanding the New Age' (£1.50)

'Raging Waves' (£4.00)
(Studies in Jude)

'Cunningly Devised Fables' (£6.50)
(a look at 13 cults and religions and
an overview of their characteristics)

Books available from:
31, Fairmeadows,
Maesteg,
South Wales, CF34 9JL.

(Prices include postage and packing)

About the Author...

Paul Young comes from Maesteg, South Wales and is married to Alison. He earned his initial degree at the University of Wales, Aberystwyth and he has since done a Masters in Theology through distance learning. Having taught at Secondary School level for six years Paul has devoted himself to full time Christian ministry since 1981. Much of his work is with his local church in Maesteg, preaching, teaching and children's ministry, along with going into schools, as well as travelling both throughout the United Kingdom and to many countries overseas for ministry. He does a regular radio programme with Trans World Radio ('Truth for Today') and has written nine books and contributed articles to a number of publications.